BLACK STORIES MATTER

AMAZING ARTISTS

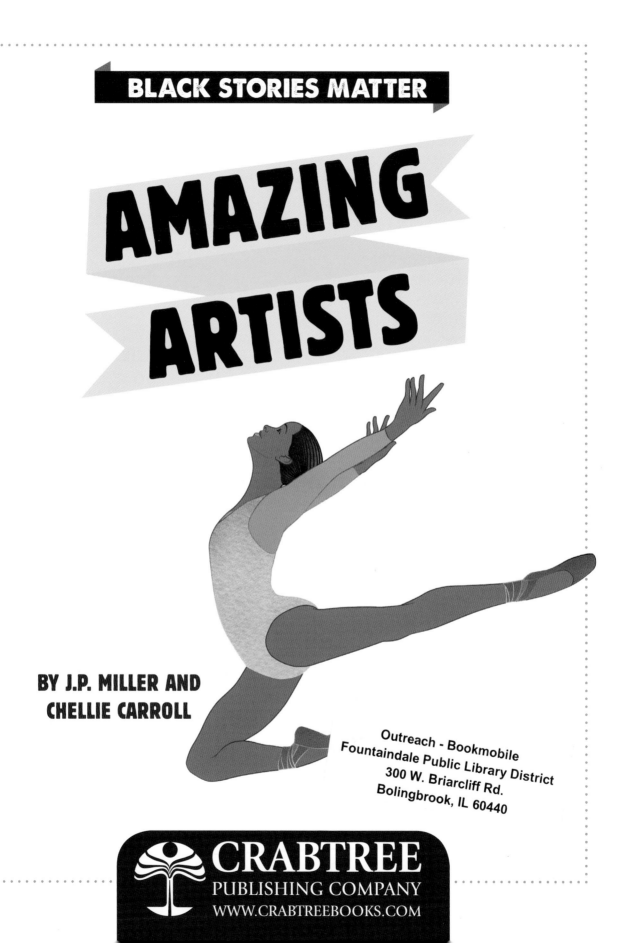

BY J.P. MILLER AND
CHELLIE CARROLL

CRABTREE
PUBLISHING COMPANY
WWW.CRABTREEBOOKS.COM

CRABTREE
PUBLISHING COMPANY
WWW.CRABTREEBOOKS.COM

Author: J.P. Miller

Editorial director: Kathy Middleton

Series editor: Julia Bird

Editor: Ellen Rodger

Designer: Peter Scoulding

Artist: Chellie Carroll

Proofreader: Petrice Custance

Production coordinator and
  Prepress technician: Tammy McGarr

Print coordinator: Katherine Berti

Library and Archives Canada Cataloguing in Publication

Title: Amazing artists / by J.P. Miller and Chellie Carroll.
Names: Miller, J. P. (Janice P.), author. | Carroll, Chellie, illustrator.
Description: Series statement: Black stories matter | Illustrated by
  Chellie Carroll. | Originally published: London : Wayland, 2020. |
  Includes bibliographical references and index.
Identifiers: Canadiana (print) 20200370219 |
  Canadiana (ebook) 20200370340 |
  ISBN 9781427128072 (hardcover) |
  ISBN 9781427128119 (softcover) |
  ISBN 9781427128157 (HTML)
Subjects: LCSH: Artists, Black—Biography—Juvenile literature. |
  LCSH: Arts, Black—Juvenile literature. | LCGFT: Biographies.
Classification: LCC NX164.B55 M55 2021 | DDC j700.92/396—dc23

Library of Congress Cataloging-in-Publication Data

Names: Miller, J. P. (Janice P.), author. | Carroll, Chellie, illustrator.
Title: Amazing artists / by J.P. Miller and Chellie Carroll.
Description: New York, NY : Crabtree Publishing Company, 2021. |
  Series: Black stories matter |
  Includes bibliographical references and index.
Identifiers: LCCN 2020047977 (print) | LCCN 2020047978 (ebook)
  ISBN 9781427128072 (hardcover) |
  ISBN 9781427128119 (paperback) |
  ISBN 9781427128157 (ebook)
Subjects: LCSH: Artists, Black--Biography--Juvenile literature.
Classification: LCC NX164.B55 M55 2021 (print) |
  LCC NX164.B55 (ebook) | DDC 700.92/2 [B]--dc23
LC record available at https://lccn.loc.gov/2020047977
LC ebook record available at https://lccn.loc.gov/2020047978

Crabtree Publishing Company
www.crabtreebooks.com   1-800-387-7650

Published in 2021 by Crabtree Publishing Company

Published in Canada
Crabtree Publishing
616 Welland Ave.
St. Catharines, Ontario
L2M 5V6

Published in the United States
Crabtree Publishing
347 Fifth Avenue
Suite 1402–145
New York, NY 10016

Printed in the U.S.A./022021/CG20201123

First published in Great Britain in 2020 by Wayland
Copyright © Hodder and Stoughton, 2020

CONTENTS

JEAN-MICHEL BASQUIAT

UNTITLED

It was once just a blank canvas. One of many used by Jean-Michel Basquiat in his Lower Manhattan, New York art studio. It came to be known as *Untitled*.

BORN:
December 22, 1960– August 12, 1988

NATIONALITY:
American

OCCUPATION: Artist

Jean-Michel lined the blank canvases against the walls. Pounding hip-hop beats in the background pumped him up to work. Their messages influenced what he painted.

"I don't think about art while I work. I try to think about life."

Jean-Michel gathered his brushes and mixed colors. As he worked, he chewed on a wad of gum and danced from one canvas to the next. Dipping. Stroking. Painting. Reaching up high to cover the edges of his edgy paintings, Jean-Michel allowed the paint from his brush to drip, splatter, and smear onto his clothes.

Effortlessly, one piece began to take form. On the center of his azure blue background Jean-Michel painted a large black skull. Bold red, white, and gold brushstrokes served as accents. A math formula crowned the top. Below were random letters written in black, then crossed out. He intentionally left the piece untitled.

Jean-Michel moved freely about his studio. He stopped to paint his signature three-pointed crown on one canvas. On another he doodled, in a style similar to the graffiti he spray painted as a teen.

The Neo-Expressionist art **movement** of the 1970s and 80s heavily influenced Jean-Michel Basquiat. Black icons and culture were his topics of choice, as were things that reflected his rich Haitian/ Puerto Rican heritage.

"The Black person is the protagonist [main character] in most of my paintings. I realized that I don't see many paintings with Black people in them."

By his early 20s, Jean-Michel had established himself as one of the most exciting new young artists and worked with industry greats such as Andy Warhol. Barefoot and dressed in a paint-smeared Giorgio Armani suit, he graced the cover of *New York* magazine in 1985. The article "NEW ART, NEW MONEY: The Making of an American Artist" described Jean-Michel's life and rapid rise to fame. Few could have predicted his untimely death just three years later.

When the gavel landed at a 2016 auction, Jean-Michel's *Untitled* stunned the world by selling for US$110.5 million. It was the most expensive piece of art ever sold by an American artist.

In his short lifetime, Jean-Michel Basquiat created a legacy that cannot be duplicated. His unique artwork is today revered all over the world.

TONI MORRISON

VOICE OF THE SOUL

BORN:
February 18, 1931
–August 5, 2019

NATIONALITY:
American

OCCUPATION:
Writer

Toni Morrison believed in the power of storytelling. As a book editor and author, she gave life to the stories and histories—real and fictional—of Black people in America. Early on, Toni realized that Black people were often portrayed in books from a White point of view. Her works helped change that.

"Every Black child in literature or theatre was a joke, a pet…or a Topsy like in *Uncle Tom's Cabin*." Writer Toni Morrison urged people: "…Pay attention to this child. Maybe she's in difficulty. She's obviously hurt. She's abused and misused. Take her seriously, please."

Through her writing, Toni unearthed the African American experience. She gave names to some of the pain and disappointments. Toni became the voice of the soul for Black people in America, and especially for women.

While her first novel was still just a seed in her mind, Toni championed the right for Black people to tell their own stories. She was the first Black female senior editor at Random House publishers. This gave her some control over how Black people were depicted, or portrayed.

Toni made deliberate, or purposeful, choices in which books she wanted to publish. For the first time, Black people, such as the boxer Muhammad Ali or the **activist** Angela Davis, were able to speak their truth through their biographies.

"I want the voices documented. I don't want them distorted by columnists… I want THEM to say what they say."

While developing books that represented Black lives, and editing the works of Black authors, Toni was also writing her own.

Toni was a multitasker. Along with her full-time job she was a single parent to her two sons, Harold and Slade. Sometimes things got a little crazy around dinner time. Toni moved hurriedly from the oven to the table to check on the boys' homework.

She often stopped to scribble in her notepad. Story ideas and inspiration could come at any time.

Toni's first novel, *The Bluest Eye*, was published in 1970, followed by *Sula* and *Songs of Solomon*. Toni was finally at a place where she could do the two things that she loved best—mother her children and write books.

Toni walked away from her job in publishing, and continued to teach and to write books and plays.

"I only write the type of books I want to read."

In 1987, Toni penned her most well-known book, *Beloved*. In it she challenged every mother to consider what they would do or how far they would go to protect their child. Her reputation as an author grew.

In 1993, Toni Morrison was presented with the **Nobel Prize** for Literature. She was the first African American woman to receive the award. In 2012, Toni was awarded the Presidential Medal of Honor by U.S. President Barack Obama, in recognition of her rich contribution to American culture.

9

STEVE MCQUEEN

DISCOVERING THE WORLD THROUGH FILM

ACT ONE
INTERIOR: UNNAMED CINEMA, NIGHT

People surround the young couple on all sides. They are unaware. The only light is the one that shines onto the silver screen. They hold hands tightly as the film keeps them captivated.

BORN:
October 9, 1969

NATIONALITY:
British

OCCUPATION: Film director and artist

It is the first time that filmmaker Steve McQueen's interest in film is **piqued**. Through the art of film, he discovers the world.

"Going to the cinema, I discovered these different worlds. I learned how people in Japan fell in love... How people ate in Taiwan... How people did things in Italy."

ACT TWO
INTERIOR: LIVING ROOM OF FAMILY HOME, WEST LONDON, DAY

Young Steve turns his focus from art and design to filmmaking. His father tries to discourage him. He hasn't seen other Black people doing what Steve wants to do. To his father, a bricklayer, filmmaking is too risky. It's not the type of career a man can support a wife and family with. He tells Steve to consider a **trade**.

ACT THREE
EXTERIOR: GOLDSMITH'S COLLEGE ART DEPT, DAY

Steve chooses to follow his passion. He has already directed a few short films and has a keen eye for **cinematography**. Steve enters Goldsmiths College, University of London to build upon that experience. At university Steve discovers art and life at the same time. He finds freedom. It is a freedom that carries over into his career.

It's this freedom that gives Steve McQueen the courage to produce short films and feature films that raise political, racial, and **gender** awareness. It allows him to peel back the scab of slavery in the United States to tell the true story of Solomon Northup in the film *12 Years a Slave*.

Act four
EXTERIOR: PORCH OF MANSION, DAY

Steve McQueen directs the actors. "Quiet on the set!"

It is the year 1841. Solomon Northup, a Black musician and free man, is sitting on a porch in Saratoga Springs, New York with two well-dressed White men. The men offer Solomon a business deal to go with them to Washington, DC to perform his music. But on his arrival, Solomon is served a dinner that makes him ill.

CUT.

Act five
INTERIOR: DARK DUNGEON, DAY.

Solomon awakes the next morning stripped of his freedom. He is in shackles. Solomon has been tricked, drugged, sold, and forced into slavery. He will be enslaved for 12 long years.

Act six
INTERIOR: OSCARS CEREMONY, LOS ANGELES, NIGHT

Actor Will Smith announces the Oscar nominees for 2014 Best Picture. The drums roll. He opens the envelope. "And the Oscar goes to...*12 Years a Slave*!"

Steve McQueen wins Best Picture for *12 Years a Slave*. Through a movie, Steve McQueen brought to life a story of enslavement few people knew. It made his name known throughout the world. In 2020, Steve McQueen, who battled **dyslexia** and **institutional racism** in school as a child, is knighted by the Queen of England for his services to film.

"It has to be a situation where you're telling a story and where the audiences trust you..."

NINA SIMONE

THE PRIESTESS OF SOUL

The house lights were low. A spotlight lit the piano. Eunice Kathleen Waymon, known by her stage name, Nina Simone, sat in front of the microphone. She waited for the audience to be quiet before she played or sang her first note.

"I don't touch the piano until they are ready to listen. I just sit there and make them wait."

BORN:
February 21, 1933–
April 21, 2003

NATIONALITY:
American

OCCUPATION:
Musician

A musical **prodigy** from childhood, Nina Simone found herself playing and singing jazz in Atlantic City supper clubs for a living. It was far from her dream of becoming a classical pianist—a dream denied because she was not accepted to a prestigious music school, despite a stellar audition.

"It haunts me!...I still wish I had been a classical pianist. But I don't look back. I am what I am."

But soon Nina's unique, soulful musical style made her a star. She signed her first record deal at 24 and never looked back.

"I Loves You Porgy" was the first of many of Nina's hit songs, and she went on to record over 40 albums.

Nina's music was partly inspired by her heritage. She was angered by violence against Black people. She sang about it. Her music became part of the soundtrack of the **civil rights movement**. Nina became active in the movement, too.

Nina was especially angered by the assassination, or targeted political murder, of **civil rights** activist Medgar Evers, and the bombing of 13th Street Baptist Church in Birmingham that killed four children. She performed at the Selma to Montgomery protest marches and supported civil rights activists Dr. Martin Luther King Jr. and Malcolm X whenever and wherever she could. "Music has helped me defend the rights of American Blacks…When I'm on stage, I make the audience conscious of what's been done."

Nina Simone energized the next generation of freedom fighters at a concert at the Morehouse, a historically Black college in Atlanta, Georgia. She sang and played her song "To Be Young, Gifted and Black." An all-male band accompanied her.

Each time Nina repeated the refrain, the crowd of young people at the concert cheered louder. They loved hearing a woman who knew what it meant to be young, gifted, and Black sing to them about being proud and joyful in who they were.

The song was a powerful tribute to her friend, the late playwright Lorraine Hansberry. It became a rallying call.

By 1965 Malcolm X had been killed. On April 4, 1968, the world learned of the assassination of Dr. Martin Luther King Jr., at the hands of a **White supremacist**. Nina wrote a heartfelt tribute for her friend and fearless leader, declaring "The king of love is dead."

Nina lost her zeal for the civil rights movement. She had taken her message of brutality and injustice toward Blacks to prominent White-only concert halls and performed for some of the world's wealthiest people. Yet the **discrimination** persisted.

So Nina moved away. The high priestess of soul left America for good. She died at her home in France. Nina received many honors in her lifetime and was inducted into the Rock and Roll Hall of Fame for her R&B work in 2018.

MALORIE BLACKMAN

BRIDGING THE DIVIDE

Writers are always on the lookout for their next story idea. A message on a billboard or bits of a passing conversation can serve as inspiration. For British author Malorie Blackman, it was headline news that helped inspire her to write the popular young adult book, *Noughts and Crosses*.

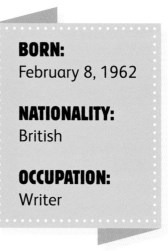

BORN:
February 8, 1962

NATIONALITY:
British

OCCUPATION:
Writer

Protest chants. Demonstration signs. Police in riot gear.
Those were the images that hit the news. Those were the scenes that followed the racially motivated attack and murder of Black teenager Stephen Lawrence in April 1993. Lawrence was stabbed to death by a group of five White men while he was waiting at night for a bus. The men had previously been involved in other racist attacks.

> "I just remember seeing how the Lawrence family had been treated by the police. They did not take the family seriously."

Britain and its leaders were being forced to confront the racism that existed in its communities.

Malorie found the painful events gave her a chance to confront a difficult topic in her writing and turn it into something her readers could learn from. But what approach would she take?

> "I need to do this in such a way people won't expect."

The story began to take form in Malorie's mind. The idea for a **superior** and **inferior** race started to come alive. The two groups competed for power in her head, each trying to persuade Malorie to tell the story their way. She quickly gained control.

Malorie sat at her computer and typed an outline. She developed a beginning, middle, and end. Malorie created a society turned on its head. The Crosses (darker-skinned) were the superior race and the Noughts (lighter-skinned) were the inferior race. Next, the real work began for Malorie...writing.

In the book, Malorie played with people's assumptions of race in an alternative 21st-century Britain. It worked. Not only was *Noughts and Crosses* a huge success, but Malorie was later able to develop its story and characters into a five-book series.

Eighteen long years passed before the Lawrence family received justice for Stephen. The process was slow, but not impossible. People such as Malorie Blackman played a role in Britain's healing. She took a tragedy and turned it into a chance to learn.

Noughts and Crosses was read by thousands of schoolchildren. It helped teen readers to understand and bridge the gap of racial difference. It was later named one of the 100 most influential English-language novels.

For her outstanding achievement in the field of children's literature, Malorie Blackman received many honors. *Noughts and Crosses* was adapted into a stage play entitled *Black & White*. In 2020, *Noughts and Crosses* was made into a television series in Britain.

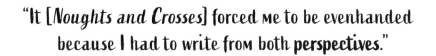

"It [*Noughts and Crosses*] forced me to be evenhanded because I had to write from both **perspectives**."

SIDNEY POITIER

AUDITION OF A LIFETIME

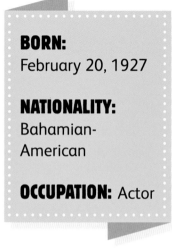

BORN:
February 20, 1927

NATIONALITY:
Bahamian-
American

OCCUPATION: Actor

One newspaper ad changed his life forever. Born in Miami to Bahamian parents, Sidney Poitier moved from the Bahamas to Harlem, New York when he was 16 years old. Every day he searched the want ads for a job.

One day Sidney spotted this ad in a newspaper:

Wanted! Theater seeking Negro actors.

Sidney had no acting experience. In fact, he had only gone to the movies once or twice in his whole life, with friends back home in the Bahamas. But it had been enough for the young Sidney to know that he wanted to be an actor.

Sidney failed miserably at his first audition. He stumbled over the lines to the script. His thick Bahamian accent made it difficult for him to be understood. But he wanted to be an actor more than anything.

So Sidney made a deal with the director: "I'll do the janitor work for free if you let me come in and study."

Sidney cleaned the stage and set up the props as promised at the American Negro Theater. Anything he was asked to do, he did. But mostly he watched and learned from the other actors.

Six months later, Sidney auditioned again. He nailed it! The audition changed his life forever. He was cast into the leading role of the Broadway play *Lysistrata*. The production wasn't a success, but it was enough to get Sidney his next role as a **understudy** in a production of *Anna Lucasta*.

21

But Hollywood and superstardom called. In 1950 Sidney was cast in the leading role in the crime drama *No Way Out*. His breakthrough role as a high school student in *Blackboard Jungle* followed in 1955. Each role from there on became increasingly more prominent and **controversial**.

When Sidney Poitier arrived in Hollywood, Black actors were mostly playing small roles in films. They were the musicians, porters, waiters, maids, and convicts.

Sidney came from a culture in the Bahamas where Blacks made up 90 percent of the population and had more power in their daily lives. He had a strong sense of self and refused to play demeaning roles.

Sidney's presence in Hollywood forged a new path for Black actors. Most of his movies dealt with race relations head-on. His 1967 box office hit *Guess Who's Coming to Dinner?* addressed interracial marriage.

Sidney was also known for sharing the first on-screen kiss between a Black man and a White woman in *A Patch of Blue*. Every character Sidney Poitier played made a statement.

It took $240,000 and 13 days to film *Lilies of the Field*. It only took Sidney Poitier ten seconds to reach the stage to receive his 1964 Oscar Award for Best Actor. He was the first Black male actor to win the award. All because he responded to a wanted ad and refused to give up on an audition.

"The laws in America said that you will be treated as less than.... I could never adjust to that."

BEYONCÉ AND JAY-Z

BEY + JAY-Z = THE CARTERS

Bey

The family loaded up the car and headed to the school. The Knowles family were used to Beyoncé singing and dancing at home. But this was their first time watching their baby girl perform on stage. That night, Beyoncé broke though her shell and emerged as an entertainer.

BORN:
September 4, 1981

NATIONALITY:
American

OCCUPATION:
Musician

Beyoncé's first major break was on the American hit talent show *Star Search*. She was one of six in the Houston, Texas all-girl group, Girl's Tyme. They didn't win, but the show was a big confidence booster. Girl's Tyme went back to Houston, regrouped, and came back as Destiny's Child.

With Beyoncé singing lead, Destiny's Child created battle cries in the late 1990s and early 2000s that flooded the airways. Songs such as "Bills, Bills, Bills" and "Independent Women" empowered women and made Beyoncé and her bandmates, Michelle Williams and Kelly Rowland, household names.

In 2003, Beyoncé released her first solo album, *Dangerously In Love*. The album got her fans, known as the Bey Hive, buzzing. Those fans helped to carry young Beyoncé's dream all the way from Houston to the Grammy Awards.

"I always try to be myself. Ever since I was an introverted kid, I'd get on stage and be able to break out of my shell."

Jay-Z

The beats would not let him sleep. Shawn Carter sat at his family's kitchen table, tapping rhythms long into the night.

By age 11, Shawn (aka Jay-Z) was deep into the East Coast rap game in Brooklyn, New York. His lyrics were fresh and unique. Jay-Z made sure of that by studying the dictionary.

Jay-Z tried everything to get out of the tough Marcy Projects housing complex where he grew up, and into the music industry. He could never get the right break. When money got tight, Jay-Z went back to what he knew best. He turned to the streets to hustle up fast money.

In 1997, on tour with rapper Puff Daddy, Jay-Z heard a beat he couldn't resist. The DJ had combined the beat with the chorus of a song from the hit Broadway musical *Annie*. Jay-Z dropped his own lyrics onto what would become "Hard Knock Life" and recorded the song on his newly established Def Jam label.

BORN:
December 4, 1969

NATIONALITY:
American

OCCUPATION:
Musician, entrepreneur

The song put Jay-Z on the national stage. "Hard Knock Life" was number one for five weeks, sold five million copies, and won Jay-Z his first Grammy award.

As his status grew, Jay-Z worked with musical greats from Rihanna to Kanye West. He became an **entrepreneur**, too. He invested in, or became part owner of, Roc-A-Fella Records, Rocawear, the Brooklyn Nets basketball team, and much more.

"I've always given parts of me, parts of my life—good, bad, ugly."

The Carters

Hip-hop's power couple met in the early 2000s. Beyoncé Knowles and Jay-Z were married on April 8, 2008. The couple added to their family in 2012 when their daughter Blue Ivy was born. In 2017, they welcomed twins, Sir and Rumi. The musical superstars are now among the richest and most powerful couples in the world.

OSCAR PETERSON

CANADA'S GIFT TO JAZZ

BORN:
August 15, 1925–
December 23, 2007

NATIONALITY: Canadian

OCCUPATION: Musician

The trio had just started their set. Oscar Peterson's fingers gently caressed the keys of the baby grand piano. A unique jazz sound flowed through New York's Carnegie Hall.

Live concerts can be unpredictable.
Some audiences are quiet,
especially when the artist is new.
Not this one.
Hands clapped…
Fingers snapped…
Heads bobbed.
Oscar's music was as relaxing as water flowing over river rocks. As bold as a hot cup of black coffee.

"You can't just sit down and play the piano.
You have to think of phrases, colors, intensities…I have to become the piano."

Oscar was winning over new fans south of the border. He was described as "Canada's gift to jazz" and later was known as the "the king of inside swing."

Growing up in Montreal, Quebec, Oscar had little time for anything other than music. His father believed that it was the only way his children could escape poverty. All five of the Peterson children learned to play instruments. They formed a family band and played at churches and social events.

Oscar did not have to go far for piano lessons. His older sister Daisy was his first piano teacher and number one fan. It was Daisy who convinced Oscar to enter a national amateur talent contest sponsored by the Canadian Broadcasting Corporation (CBC). At age 15, Oscar won the Junior Division. Afterward, he became a regular on the Montreal hit radio show *Fifteen Minutes Piano Rambling* and the CBC broadcast *The Happy Gang*.

The Johnny Holmes Orchestra was the most popular jazz band in Montreal. Oscar became its newest member. He was the first Black Canadian to join the band. But already his career in jazz was reaching new heights. So were his life experiences.

One evening, the Johnny Holmes Orchestra had a big gig at the Montreal Ritz Hotel. The hotel had a policy of not allowing Black performers on their stage. So Oscar took a back seat and encouraged the band to play without him. Sadly, this was just one instance of the racism that Oscar would encounter throughout his career.

One of Oscar's most important relationships was with his manager, Norman Granz. The story goes that Norman heard Oscar playing on the radio while he was in a taxi heading to a Montreal airport. He told the driver to turn around and take him to meet the talented young pianist. He became Oscar's manager for most of his career.

Oscar was a multiple Grammy Award winner and a regular at jazz festivals around the world throughout his six-decade-long career in music. He believed strongly in the importance of jazz education. Oscar ran a school, the Advanced School of Contemporary Music, from 1960 to 1964. He also became a professor of Music at York University in 1986.

"Nothing takes the place of music for me.
That's my first and foremost love."

MISTY COPELAND

I BELONG HERE

"Quiet on the set!" commanded the director, Georgia Hudson. Two chords played softly on the piano. Dancer Misty Copeland stood stage left awaiting her next cue. She was on set filming a commercial for the Under Armour clothing company. A child's voice heard over the music says:

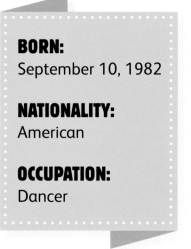

BORN:
September 10, 1982

NATIONALITY:
American

OCCUPATION:
Dancer

"Dear Candidate,
Thank you for your application to our ballet academy. Unfortunately, you have not been accepted. You have the wrong body for ballet…"

Although this rejection letter was written only for the commercial, Misty recalled receiving letters such as this herself that were equally harsh. Misty was considered an unlikely ballerina because she was Black and because she started ballet late, at age 13. But she danced past the critics, all the while saying to herself, "I belong here."

Misty took her first ballet lesson at the San Pedro Boys and Girls Club in California. She was **en pointe** three months later—an astonishing achievement. She went on to win competitions and join a ballet company.

"Something happens when you feel the energy and excitement from the audience…you do four pirouettes and jump higher than you ever have."

Misty danced her way to the **prestigious** American Ballet Theater in New York. But with her success came loneliness…then depression. Misty did not feel as if she belonged there.

> "It hit me once I moved to New York…I was the only African-American in a company of eighty dancers."

Misty grew into womanhood before the ballet company's eyes. In a matter of months she gained 11 pounds (5 kg). Curves outlined her body and her muscles showed their strength. Misty developed a muscular physique that was rarely seen in the dance world.

As a ballet dancer, there was pressure on Misty to lose weight and to look a certain way. Misty started to struggle with her body image. She even thought of pursuing something other than ballet.

The American Ballet Theater asked one of its board members, Susan Fales-Hill, to mentor Misty. Susan introduced her to other African American female trailblazers, such as actress Diahann Carroll, model Veronica Webb, and Raven Wilkinson, the first African American woman to dance for a major classical ballet company. They all became Misty's support. They helped her to understand that she had the same ability they had to break glass ceilings and realize her huge potential.

Misty regained focus. Her ballet career was back en pointe. The American Ballet Theater promoted her to soloist and later, principal ballerina. She became the first African American woman to hold the title of principal ballerina in the ballet company's history. Misty Copeland belonged there.

Misty's role is more than dancer. She is now an influencer who works to **diversify** the dance world.

STEVIE WONDER

A BRIDGE TO RACE RELATIONS

BORN:
May 13, 1950

NATIONALITY:
American

OCCUPATION:
Musician

The snap, crackle, and pop of breakfast was put on hold. Stevie Wonder was up next on the American children's TV series *Sesame Street*. Stevie and his entire band were there to perform his hit song "Superstition."

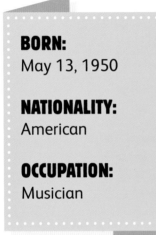

A group of school-age children shook maracas, banged their tambourines, and danced. The producers were deliberately showing ethnic diversity. It was 1973 and the U.S. was still adapting to **integrated** schools, where Black and White children learned together.

Stevie Wonder was the biggest musical act to perform on the show up to that point. His R&B, funk, and jazz-infused sound helped win Stevie a new fan base. With crossover hits such as "For Once in My Life," "Living For the City," and "My Cherie Amour," Stevie Wonder became a bridge to closer race relations between Black and White people.

> "If we don't correct the things that keep us in a certain place we will not move forward."

Little Stevland Morris from Saginaw, Michigan had come a long way. Though visually impaired at birth, Stevland never thought of himself as being disabled. He went from being a harmonica-playing eleven-year-old to the musical hitmaker, Stevie Wonder.

In the 1970s, Stevie Wonder used his stardom to join Coretta Scott King, the widow of the great Black activist, Dr. Martin Luther King Jr., in her campaign to make her late husband's birthday a national holiday. He campaigned tirelessly for the holiday until it was passed into law in 1982.

Stevie wasn't finished with activism. He directed his attention to South Africa, which was at that time ruled by a White government which used a system of **segregation** called apartheid that allowed White citizens to dominate non-White citizens.

In 1985, Stevie Wonder won an Academy Award for Best Original Song in a Movie for his hit song, "I Just Called to Say I Love You" from the film *The Woman in Red.*

In his acceptance speech, Stevie seemingly made an innocent dedication: "I would like to accept this award in the name of Nelson Mandela."

Stevie had pledged his support for Nelson Mandela, the imprisoned leader of the African National Party, which was fighting against apartheid in South Africa. Stevie's music was later banned from all South African radio stations by the government.

Stevie Wonder has continued to release hit songs for more than 50 years. He also continues to work with organizations that are dedicated to helping people with disabilities and fighting against poverty and racism.

In 2009, Stevie was made a Messenger of Peace by the United Nations, an international organization that works to promote peace and security.

"What I'm not confused about is the world needing much more love, no hate, no prejudice, no bigotry, and more unity, peace, and understanding..."

Read on to find out more about some other amazing Black artists, both past and present.

COMMON

There is nothing common about Lonnie Corant Jaman Shuka Rashid Lynn Jr., the rapper, actor, writer, and activist better known as Common. He hit the rap scene in 1992 and riddled the 1990s and 2000s with hits. Between hip hop and movie roles, the rapper uses his voice to address issues in Black America.

BORN:
March 13, 1972

NATIONALITY:
American

OCCUPATION:
Musician, actor, activist

> *"One of the most important things I learned about being a leader is being a servant."*

Common is very vocal on the **incarceration** of Black men. He was a contributor to Ava DuVernay's 2016 documentary *13th*, which looks at the loophole in the 13th Amendment of the U.S. constitution that legalizes the imprisonment of Black boys and men.

Common has taken his passion back home to Chicago with his Common Ground Foundation. He gives his time and resources to help give inner city youths a sense of hope.

CHIMAMANDA NGOZI ADICHIE

BORN:
September 15, 1977

NATIONALITY:
Nigerian

OCCUPATION:
Writer

As a child, Chimamanda Ngozi Adichie was an excellent student. When she wasn't doing school work, Chimamanda always had a book in her hands. She loved to read. Most of the books Chimamanda read were written by American or British authors. Although she enjoyed reading them, the books did not have characters that looked, sounded, or lived like Chimamanda.

In primary school, Chimamanda realized that Africa and its people were not shown authentically in books. She pursued writing to change that. She wanted to write stories in her own voice, as one who was from Nigeria, living amongst Nigerian cultures. Through her books, readers are introduced to the real-life languages and customs of her homeland. Chimamanda is best known for her award-winning book *Purple Hibiscus* (2003).

IDRIS ELBA

Idris Elba has swagger! He has that keen sense of fashion and confidence that makes him stand out, and gives him a charismatic screen presence.

Idris felt he was too skinny when he was a young man. He started kickboxing to develop his body. By the time he left the U.K. to pursue his dream of acting in America, Idris was physically and artistically ready for the silver screen. His big break came playing drug overlord Russell "Stringer" Bell in the popular TV series *The Wire*. His other starring roles include *The Jungle Book*, *Mandela: Long Walk to Freedom*, *Avengers: Infinity War* and more. When he's not acting, Idris campaigns for more diversity on-screen.

BORN:
September 6, 1972

NATIONALITY:
British/Sierra Leonean

OCCUPATION:
Actor

LANGSTON HUGHES

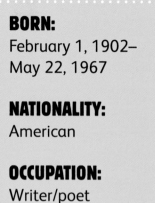

BORN:
February 1, 1902–
May 22, 1967

NATIONALITY:
American

OCCUPATION:
Writer/poet

The streets were packed. Clubs too. Many African Americans left the South and moved to Harlem, New York for more freedom and opportunity. The Great Migration (1916–1970) brought six million Blacks to northern cities. Segregation and discrimination still existed in the North, but there was less fear and intimidation. Amidst this, in the 1920s, a cultural revolution took place, and poet Langston Hughes was one of its leading lights.

Harlem became a hub of Black culture and a home to writers, poets, artists, and musicians during a period called the Harlem Renaissance (1910–1930s). Langston Hughes wrote poems, such as "My People" (1923), which tackled segregation and the Black experience head-on. He wrote of pride in Blackness and Black cultures. During his lifetime, Langston Hughes won countless awards for his poems, novels, plays, and short stories.

LUPITA NYONG'O

BORN:
March 1, 1983

NATIONALITY:
Kenyan/Mexican

OCCUPATION:
Actor/producer

It takes an exceptional performance, and phenomenal box office earnings, to win awards in Hollywood's entertainment industry. The rock star success of the films *12 Years a Slave, Black Panther,* and *Us* did just that for the Mexico-born Kenyan actor Lupita Nyong'o. In her film debut, Lupita won an Academy Award for Best Actress in a Supporting Role for her portrayal of Patsey in *12 Years a Slave.*

As a child, Lupita Nyong'o performed regularly with her family at gatherings. It wasn't until she saw Whoopi Goldberg star in the acclaimed film *The Color Purple* that she took acting more seriously and saw it as a possible career. She later graduated with a master's degree in acting from Yale University and launched a career that has seen her also become a representative of empowerment. Lupita speaks out for causes she believes in, including nature conservation. She also published a children's picture book, *Sulwe.* It encourages young readers to find beauty in all skin colors.

NIKKI GIOVANNI

BORN:
June 7, 1943

NATIONALITY:
American

OCCUPATION:
Poet

When poet Nikki Giovanni steps up to the microphone the crowd listens with delight. Nikki's poetry grooves…it soothes …it makes one think.

Nikki speaks her truth. Sharing wisdom with youth.

For five decades, Nikki Giovanni has inspired the world with her soul-stirring poetry. She was one of the voices of the Black Arts Movement (BAM) of the 1960s and 70s. BAM emphasized pride in Black culture and forms of cultural expression. Nikki's earlier pieces were heavily influenced by the civil rights movement.

For her work, Nikki Giovanni has been honored with numerous awards, including the prestigious National Association for the Advancement of Colored People (NAACP) Image Award for Outstanding Literary Work.

EDMONIA LEWIS

Patience, a sharp eye, and a steady hand were Edmonia Lewis's best qualities. It took her four years to complete her most famous sculpture, *The Death of Cleopatra*. Edmonia Lewis was one of the best in the field and the first woman of African American and Indigenous descent to receive international recognition for her sculpting.

Edmonia's studio was filled with clay models used to make her marble pieces. She moved back and forth from the clay to the marble, taking measurements. She had to be precise in her calculations or risk making a defective piece. Edmonia chiseled, sanded, and polished until she reached perfection.

Born in Greenbush, New York, Edmonia spent much of her adult life in Rome, Italy. The first professional African American sculptor, she found more artistic freedom there. One of her best-known sculptures, *Forever Free,* shows a Black man and woman at the moment they are freed from slavery.

BORN:
July 4, 1844–
September 17, 1907

NATIONALITY:
American

OCCUPATION:
Sculptor

AMY SHERALD

The crowd at the National Portrait Gallery in Washington, D.C., sat anxiously in their seats.

Cameras and video recorders pointed at the 6-by-5 foot (1.8 by 1.5 m) black draped canvas before them. In one split second, the cloth was dropped.

The crowd gasped in delight at the unveiled portrait of America's first African American First Lady, Michelle Obama. Sharing the spotlight was the artist, Amy Sherald.

For some, it was their first view of the work of the Columbus, Georgia native. But Amy has been an artist for a long time. She likes to paint everyday people.

Amy paints African Americans in gray tones. She believes it shows more of their private energy. The Clark Atlanta University graduate's work can now be found in galleries all over the world.

BORN:
August 30, 1973

NATIONALITY:
American

OCCUPATION:
Painter

"I just see people and know automatically that is a person I would like to see a painting of."

GLOSSARY

activist Someone who works to bring about change

cinematography The art of shooting films

civil rights Rights and opportunities guaranteed under the law of a country to all people regardless of race, religion, or gender

civil rights movement A struggle for justice for Black people and people of color that included marches and protests that took place mainly in the 1950s and 1960s

controversial Stirring up strong opinions

discrimination To treat a person or group of people better or worse than others, often because of their gender, race, or religion

dyslexia A learning disorder that makes it difficult for people to read

diversify To make a group or society one that includes people of different races, cultures, genders, and abilities

en pointe When a dancer supports all their body weight on the tips of their toes

entrepreneur Someone who sets up a business

gender A range of identities that people identify with, such as female, male, both, or other

incarceration Being sent to prison

inferior Considered lower in rank or status

institutional racism Racism that is system wide and considered so normal that its practices, such as discrimination in housing or jobs, are not recognized, or denied as existing

integrated Something that is blended, such as when Black and White people learn or work together

movement An organized group that acts to change something

Neo-Expressionist A style of art in which people or scenes are painted in unrealistic ways in order to show emotion or make a statement

Nobel Prize An international prize awarded to recognize someone's work in their field

perspective The particular way a person views or feels about a subject

piqued Roused or stirred up interest

prestigious Something that has high status or respect

prodigy Someone who is recognized as extremely talented from a young age

segregation The system of separating White people from Black people in order to deny them equal opportunities in education, health, housing, and other areas

superior Considered higher in rank or status

trade A job that requires special training and skills

understudy A person who learns a role in order to act as a replacement

White supremacist Someone who believes White people are superior and should therefore have more power in society

LEARNING MORE

Books

Cachin, Olivier. *Black Music Greats*. Wide-Eyed Editions, 2020.

Cooke, Tim. *Working Toward Achieving Civil Rights*. Crabtree Publishing, 2020.

Websites and videos

Discover **Jean-Michel Basquiat's** art at:
www.basquiat.com

Listen to **Nina Simone** singing "Young, Gifted, and Black" live at Morehouse College at:
www.youtube.com/watch?v=_hdVFiANBTk

Watch **Misty Copeland** dance in "The Nutcracker" at:
www.youtube.com/watch?v=ga994llm96A

Walker, Robin. *Black History Matters*. Franklin Watts, 2019.

Wilson, Jamia. *Young, Gifted, and Black*. Wide-Eyed Editions, 2018.

Watch **Stevie Wonder** perform "Superstition" live on *Sesame Street* at:
www.youtube.com/watch?v=_ul7X5js1vE

Visit this site for amazing art project ideas and to learn more about Black artists:
https://artprojectsforkids.org/category/view-by-theme/black-history-month/

The website addresses (URLs) included in this book were valid at the time of printing. It is possible that contents or addresses may have changed since the publication of this book. Neither the Publisher or author accept responsibility for any changes.

QUOTE SOURCES

Jean-Michel Basquiat p. 4 "I don't think about art...": Inside Contemporary Art, May 21, 2013, https://vecchiatoart.blogspot com/2013/05/i-dont-think-about-art-while-i-work-i.html; p.5 "The black person is the protagonist...": Sutori, www.sutori.com/story/jean-michel-basquiat-the-black-picasso–2WovNUYWEMQAJP2aUZ6FXtcf. **Toni Morrison** p. 7 "Every black child in literature....": Manufacturing Intelligent, August 7, 2019, www.youtube.com/watch?v=-OURXCUdeOA (mark 9:38-9:45); p. 7 "Pay attention to this child...": Manufacturing Intelligent, August 7, 2019, www.youtube.com/watch?v=-OURXCUdeOA (mark 10:10:-10:24); p. 7 "I want the voices documented...." Manufacturing Intelligent, August 7, 2019, www.youtube.com/watch?v=-OURXCUdeOA (mark 39:29:-39:50); p. 9 "I only write....": Hoby, Hermione, April 25, 2015, www.theguardian.com/books/2015/apr/25/toni-morrison-books-interview-god-help-the-child. **Steve McQueen** p.10 "Going to the cinema...." SAG-AFTRA Foundation, December 7, 2018, www.youtube.com/watch?v=HthRkqPQfqo (mark 4:34 -4:50; p.12 "It has to be a situation...." October 25, 2013. FastCompany www.fastcompany.com/3020648/truth-is-truth-steve-mcqueen-on-making-12-years-a-slave. **Nina Simone** p.14 "I don't touch the piano...." www.youtube.com/watch?v=8olEruTT_io (mark 20:55-21:10) p.15 "It haunts me! ... " LukeK79 www.youtube.com/watch?v=d-oW1E_tAEQ (mark 6:55 – 7:09); p.15 "Music has helped me...."BBC Hard Talk, April 24, 2017,www.youtube.com/watch?v=8olEruTT_io (mark 2:45 to 3:03). **Malorie Blackman** p.18 "I just remember seeing...." VeeKativhu, March 7, 2019, www.youtube.com/watch?v=VV7d5PCBp24 (mark 1:08 – 1:16); p.18 "I need to do this...." VeeKativhu, March 7, 2019, www.youtube.com/watch?v=VV7d5PCBp24 (mark 2:30 – 2:35); p.19 "It [Noughts and Crosses] forced me...." VeeKativhu, March 7, 2019, www.youtube.com/watch?v=VV7d5PCBp24 (mark 3:35 – 3:44) **Sidney Poitier** p. 20 "I'll do the janitor work...." Memory Lane, August 22, 2019, www.youtube.com/watch?v=NaNTHMkCKs8 (mark 11:34 – 11:44) p. 22 "The laws in America said...." Memory Lane, August 22, 2019, www.youtube.com/watch?v=NaNTHMkCKs8 (mark 32:47-33:00). **Beyoncé & Jay-Z** p. 24 "I always try to be myself...." Redbook Magazine, September 22, 2009, www.redbookmag.com/body/mental-health/interviews/a5266/beyonce-knowles-interview/ p. 26 "I've always given parts of me..." Alex Bilmes, GQ Magazine (British edition), October 2005. **Oscar Peterson** p. 29 "You can't just sit down...' Montreal Gazette, "Jazz Legend Oscar Peterson Dies at 82 - Obituary," December 24, 2007, www.youtube.com/watch?v=5DESuF9Rfck; p.31: "Nothing takes the place..." Rare Jazz Videos 2, "Oscar Peterson Interview- TV From Copenhagen," August 24, 2012. Digital. **Misty Copeland** p. 32 "I belong here." WHNT News, December 14, 2014, whnt.com/2014/12/14/misty-copeland-an-unlikely-ballerina/p. 32 "Something happens when...." Bill Whitaker, May 10, 2015, www.cbsnews.com/news/misty-copeland-unlikely-ballerina-60-minutes; p. 35 "It hit me once I moved to New York ...." WHNT News, December 14, 2014, whnt.com/2014/12/14/misty-copeland-an-unlikely-ballerina. **Stevie Wonder** p. 37 "If we don't correct the things...." Larry King, February 2, 2018,www.youtube.com/watch?v=vJh-DV1v1JM (mark 0:06-0:12) p. 38 "I would like to accept this award..." Oscars, August 28, 2013, www.youtube.com/watch?v=Bhyvt3APwAE (mark 2:20-2:32) p. 38 "What I'm not confused about is..."Christine Thomasos, September 3, 2012, www.christianpost.com/trends/stevie-wonder-clarifies-comments-about-gay-people-being-confused.html. **Common** p. 40: "One of the most important things..." Miles, Keith, "FAMU Commencement Speakers Common and Gillum Urged Graduates to Serve," FAMUForward, 17 May 2010. Digital. www.famunews.com/2019/05/famu-commencement-speakers-common-and-gillum-urged-graduates-to-serve-2/. **Amy Sherald** p. 45 Kugel, Sara, "Amy Sherald on Painting 'Everyday People,' CBS Sunday Morning,October 18, 2019. Digital. www.cbsnews.com/video/amy-sherald-on-painting-everyday-people/#x

INDEX

AUTHOR AND ILLUSTRATOR BIOGRAPHIES

Black Stories Matter: Amazing Artists includes stories of Black artists from around the world. These are only a few of the people who have used their gift of artistry to break barriers in literature and the performing and visual arts. Each of them paved the way for people of color in and out of the arts to be their true selves.

J.P. Miller is a children's author with an interest in the African Diaspora. She hopes that her stories will set fire to old stereotypes and shed light on the many contributions Black people have made throughout the world. J.P. lives in Metro Atlanta, Georgia.

Chellie Carroll is an artist who shares her time with her two children, climbing crags and hills near her home in Derbyshire, U.K.